EMMANUEL JOSEPH

Next Chapter: Getting Better After Dismissal

Copyright © 2025 by Emmanuel Joseph

All rights reserved. No part of this publication may be reproduced, stored or transmitted in any form or by any means, electronic, mechanical, photocopying, recording, scanning, or otherwise without written permission from the publisher. It is illegal to copy this book, post it to a website, or distribute it by any other means without permission.

First edition

This book was professionally typeset on Reedsy.
Find out more at reedsy.com

Contents

1. Chapter 1 — 1
2. Chapter 1: Facing the Reality — 3
3. Chapter 2: Self-Reflection and Learning — 5
4. Chapter 3: Emotional Resilience — 7
5. Chapter 4: Rebuilding Confidence — 9
6. Chapter 5: Redefining Success — 11
7. Chapter 6: Skills Enhancement — 13
8. Chapter 7: Building a Strong Network — 15
9. Chapter 8: Crafting a Winning Resume — 17
10. Chapter 9: Mastering the Job Search — 19
11. Chapter 10: Thriving in the New Workplace — 21
12. Chapter 11: Financial Planning After Dismissal — 23
13. Chapter 12: Embracing the Journey — 25

1

Chapter 1

Introduction

Dismissal from a job is a pivotal moment that many people experience at least once in their professional lives. It's a moment that can be filled with a mix of emotions—shock, frustration, fear, and even relief. The journey that follows such an event is one of introspection, resilience, and growth. "Next Chapter: Getting Better After Dismissal" is a guide designed to help you navigate this challenging period, turn it into a learning experience, and emerge stronger and more determined.

The initial phase after dismissal is often the most difficult. The sense of loss can be overwhelming, as our jobs are not only a source of income but also a significant part of our identities. This book aims to address the emotional turmoil and provide practical steps to cope with the immediate aftermath. It's about understanding that while this chapter of your life has ended, it's also the beginning of a new one, filled with opportunities for growth and self-discovery.

Self-reflection plays a critical role in the process of recovery. By taking a step back and analyzing the events that led to your dismissal, you can gain valuable insights into your strengths and weaknesses. This book will guide you through a process of honest self-assessment and help you turn mistakes into learning opportunities. It's about viewing this setback as a stepping stone rather than a stumbling block.

Building emotional resilience is essential for moving forward. The ability to bounce back from adversity and maintain a positive outlook can make all the difference. This book will explore various techniques and strategies to help you build this resilience. From mindfulness practices to seeking support from friends and family, you'll find ways to strengthen your emotional fortitude and prepare for the next steps in your career.

Rebuilding confidence is another crucial aspect of recovery. After a dismissal, it's common to feel a dip in self-esteem. This book will provide practical advice on how to regain your confidence and approach new opportunities with a renewed sense of self-assurance. Setting small, achievable goals and celebrating your victories, no matter how minor, will help you rebuild your confidence and maintain a positive momentum.

Redefining success is an empowering exercise that can open new doors and possibilities. This book will encourage you to rethink traditional definitions of success and explore new career paths that align with your values and aspirations. It's about finding fulfillment and purpose in new ventures, and embracing a growth mindset that welcomes change and continuous improvement.

Networking and building a strong support system are vital components of the recovery process. This book will offer strategies for expanding your professional network and leveraging social media platforms to connect with like-minded individuals. The support of mentors, peers, and professional communities can provide valuable guidance and encouragement as you navigate your next chapter.

Finally, this book is about embracing the journey and looking forward to future opportunities with optimism and confidence. It's a reminder that dismissal is not the end but a new beginning. By focusing on personal growth, continuous learning, and maintaining a positive attitude, you can turn this challenging experience into a transformative one. "Next Chapter: Getting Better After Dismissal" is your companion on this journey, offering practical advice, emotional support, and inspiration to help you succeed.

2

Chapter 1: Facing the Reality

The moment of dismissal often hits like a ton of bricks. It's a potent mix of disbelief, anger, and fear that can leave one feeling adrift. Many of us tie our identity closely to our professional lives, so when that foundation is suddenly pulled out from under us, it's a profound shock to the system. This chapter will walk you through those initial, tumultuous emotions and help you to understand that it's a perfectly natural response. It's not just about what happened, but about recognizing the wide range of emotions that come with such a life-altering event.

Understanding the common reasons for dismissal is crucial. Whether it was due to economic downturns, company restructuring, or performance issues, it's important to see that this experience is far from unique. Countless successful individuals have faced setbacks and come out stronger. Acceptance is the first step toward healing. By acknowledging that this isn't a reflection of your personal worth, you can start to dismantle the negative self-talk that often follows a dismissal.

A significant part of moving forward involves facing your emotions head-on. Rather than suppressing feelings of sadness, frustration, or embarrassment, allow yourself to experience them fully. It might seem counterintuitive, but this process is key to emotional recovery. Bottling up emotions can lead to prolonged distress and can hinder your ability to move on. Embrace the idea that it's okay to feel vulnerable and that vulnerability is a stepping stone to resilience.

Once the initial shock has subsided, it's time to take proactive steps toward the future. Planning might feel overwhelming at first, but breaking it down into manageable tasks can make the process more approachable. Start by setting small, achievable goals that can gradually build your confidence and momentum. This chapter will guide you on creating a practical plan that not only addresses immediate concerns but also lays the groundwork for long-term success.

Lastly, remember that you don't have to navigate this journey alone. Lean on your support network of family, friends, and possibly professional counselors. Sharing your experiences and receiving encouragement can significantly lighten the emotional load. Having a solid support system can make a world of difference as you begin to rebuild and move forward. This chapter aims to instill the belief that while this is a challenging period, it's also a chapter of new beginnings.

3

Chapter 2: Self-Reflection and Learning

Self-reflection is a crucial step after experiencing dismissal. Taking time to analyze the events leading to your dismissal can provide valuable insights. It's not about placing blame but understanding what happened and why. Perhaps there were signs you missed or areas where you could have performed better. By objectively assessing the situation, you can identify the factors within your control and those that were beyond it. This introspection is the foundation for future growth.

An honest self-assessment is necessary to pinpoint areas for improvement. It requires courage to look at yourself critically, but it's essential for personal development. List your strengths and weaknesses and consider how they played a role in your dismissal. Were there skills you lacked or behaviors that hindered your performance? By identifying these areas, you can create a targeted plan for self-improvement. This chapter will guide you through a comprehensive self-assessment process.

Feedback from others can be invaluable. Seek constructive feedback from former colleagues, supervisors, or mentors who can provide an external perspective on your performance. This feedback can highlight blind spots and offer specific areas for growth. It's essential to approach this with an open mind and a willingness to learn. While it may be challenging to hear criticism, it's a powerful tool for personal and professional development.

Turning mistakes into learning opportunities is a hallmark of successful individuals. Rather than dwelling on failures, view them as stepping stones to success. Each mistake carries a lesson that can be used to avoid similar pitfalls in the future. This chapter will emphasize the importance of a growth mindset, where challenges are seen as opportunities for improvement. By adopting this perspective, you can transform setbacks into valuable learning experiences.

Creating a personal roadmap for growth and development is the final step in self-reflection. This roadmap should include specific, actionable steps to address the areas identified during your assessment. Whether it's acquiring new skills, changing behaviors, or seeking new opportunities, having a clear plan will provide direction and motivation. This chapter will help you craft a detailed roadmap that aligns with your long-term goals and aspirations.

continue

4

Chapter 3: Emotional Resilience

The emotional toll of dismissal cannot be overstated. It often triggers a cascade of stress, anxiety, and even depression. Emotional resilience is the ability to bounce back from these negative feelings and find a path forward. Building this resilience is not an overnight process; it requires consistent effort and a variety of strategies. In this chapter, we'll explore techniques such as mindfulness, meditation, and positive visualization. These practices can help you stay grounded and focused during challenging times.

Your support network plays a crucial role in fostering emotional resilience. Friends and family can provide a listening ear, offer words of encouragement, and help you maintain perspective. Don't hesitate to reach out to them when you're feeling low. Additionally, seeking professional help from a therapist or counselor can provide valuable tools for managing stress and building resilience. Remember, asking for help is a sign of strength, not weakness.

Practicing self-compassion is another key element of emotional resilience. Treat yourself with the same kindness and understanding that you would offer to a friend in a similar situation. Acknowledge your feelings without judgment and remind yourself that it's okay to struggle. Self-compassion can alleviate the burden of self-criticism and foster a more positive mindset. This chapter will offer practical exercises to cultivate self-compassion in your daily life.

Engaging in activities that bring you joy and fulfillment can also bolster emotional resilience. Hobbies, sports, and creative pursuits can provide a much-needed escape from stress and help you reconnect with your passions. Whether it's painting, gardening, or playing a musical instrument, these activities can provide a sense of accomplishment and purpose. This chapter will encourage you to rediscover and prioritize the activities that make you happy.

Lastly, maintaining a healthy lifestyle is essential for emotional resilience. Regular exercise, a balanced diet, and sufficient sleep can significantly impact your mood and energy levels. Physical activity, in particular, has been shown to reduce stress and improve mental health. This chapter will provide tips for incorporating healthy habits into your routine, helping you build the physical and emotional resilience needed to navigate this challenging period.

5

Chapter 4: Rebuilding Confidence

After a dismissal, it's common to feel a dip in self-confidence. Rebuilding this confidence is crucial for moving forward. Start by setting small, achievable goals that can restore a sense of accomplishment. These goals can be as simple as completing a daily exercise routine or learning a new skill. As you achieve these goals, you'll begin to rebuild your confidence and prove to yourself that you are capable and resilient.

Celebrating small victories is an important part of the confidence-building process. Acknowledge and reward yourself for your achievements, no matter how minor they may seem. This positive reinforcement can boost your self-esteem and motivate you to keep pushing forward. This chapter will provide practical tips for recognizing and celebrating your successes, helping you build a positive momentum.

Networking and connecting with supportive communities can also help rebuild confidence. Surround yourself with people who uplift and inspire you. Join professional groups, attend networking events, and engage with online communities related to your field. These connections can provide valuable support, feedback, and opportunities for growth. This chapter will offer strategies for building and nurturing a strong support network.

Understanding that confidence is built over time and through persistence is key. It's normal to have moments of doubt, but with consistent effort and a positive mindset, you'll gradually regain your self-assurance. This chapter will emphasize the importance of patience and perseverance in the confidence-building journey. Remember, confidence is not a destination but an ongoing process of growth and self-improvement.

Finally, this chapter will explore the concept of self-efficacy—the belief in your ability to succeed in specific situations. By focusing on your strengths and past successes, you can develop a stronger sense of self-efficacy. This chapter will provide exercises to help you identify and leverage your strengths, boosting your confidence and preparing you for future challenges.

6

Chapter 5: Redefining Success

Dismissal provides an opportunity to rethink traditional definitions of success. Success is not a one-size-fits-all concept; it varies from person to person. Take this time to explore what success truly means to you. Is it financial stability, personal fulfillment, or making a positive impact on others? This chapter will guide you through a process of redefining success in a way that aligns with your values and aspirations.

Exploring new career paths and opportunities is an exciting aspect of redefining success. Your dismissal may have closed one door, but it can open many others. Consider industries or roles you've always been curious about but never had the chance to pursue. This chapter will encourage you to think outside the box and explore unconventional career paths that align with your passions and strengths.

Aligning your personal values and goals with your professional aspirations is crucial for long-term satisfaction. Reflect on what matters most to you and how you can incorporate those values into your career. Whether it's work-life balance, creativity, or social impact, finding a career that aligns with your values can lead to greater fulfillment. This chapter will help you identify your core values and incorporate them into your career planning.

Embracing a growth mindset is essential for redefining success. A growth mindset is the belief that abilities and intelligence can be developed through dedication and hard work. This perspective allows you to view challenges as opportunities for growth rather than obstacles. This chapter will provide strategies for cultivating a growth mindset and applying it to your career journey.

Finally, this chapter will emphasize the importance of finding fulfillment and purpose in new ventures. Success is not just about achieving goals but about finding joy and meaning in the process. By focusing on activities and careers that bring you fulfillment, you can create a more satisfying and rewarding life. This chapter will offer practical tips for discovering your passions and aligning them with your professional aspirations.

7

Chapter 6: Skills Enhancement

Identifying key skills needed for career advancement is a critical step in your journey after dismissal. Consider both hard skills, such as technical abilities and industry-specific knowledge, and soft skills, such as communication, teamwork, and problem-solving. This chapter will guide you through a self-assessment to determine which skills you need to develop or enhance. Understanding your skill gaps will help you focus your efforts and make the most of your professional development opportunities.

Opportunities for further education and professional development are more accessible than ever. Online courses, workshops, and certification programs offer flexible and affordable ways to learn new skills and stay competitive in your field. This chapter will explore various resources and platforms for continuing education. Whether you're looking to deepen your expertise in your current industry or pivot to a new one, investing in your education is a valuable step toward career growth.

Leveraging online courses and workshops can provide you with the knowledge and credentials needed to advance your career. Platforms like Coursera, Udemy, and LinkedIn Learning offer a wide range of courses taught by industry experts. This chapter will provide tips for selecting the right courses and making the most of your online learning experience. By staying proactive and committed to your development, you can build a strong foundation for future success.

Practical tips for enhancing both hard and soft skills will be discussed in this chapter. For hard skills, focus on areas that are in high demand within your industry. For soft skills, seek out opportunities to practice and refine your abilities, such as joining clubs, volunteering, or participating in group projects. This chapter will provide actionable steps for skill enhancement, helping you become a well-rounded and competitive candidate in the job market.

Keeping up with industry trends and innovations is essential for staying relevant in your field. Subscribe to industry publications, attend conferences, and follow thought leaders on social media to stay informed about the latest developments. This chapter will emphasize the importance of continuous learning and staying adaptable in an ever-changing job market. By staying current, you'll be better prepared to seize new opportunities and advance your career.

8

Chapter 7: Building a Strong Network

The importance of professional networking cannot be overstated. Building a strong network can open doors to new opportunities, provide valuable insights, and offer support during challenging times. This chapter will explore the various benefits of networking and how to approach it strategically. Whether you're attending events, joining professional organizations, or leveraging social media, networking is a key component of career success.

Strategies for building and maintaining meaningful connections will be discussed in this chapter. Start by reaching out to former colleagues, mentors, and industry contacts. Attend networking events and industry conferences to meet new people and expand your network. This chapter will provide tips for making a positive impression, following up with contacts, and nurturing long-term relationships. Building a strong network requires effort and consistency, but the rewards are well worth it.

Leveraging social media and professional platforms like LinkedIn can significantly enhance your networking efforts. Create a compelling LinkedIn profile that highlights your skills, experience, and accomplishments. Engage with industry-related content, join relevant groups, and participate in discussions to increase your visibility. This chapter will offer practical advice for using social media to build and maintain your professional network.

The role of mentorship in personal and career growth cannot be underestimated. A mentor can provide guidance, support, and valuable insights based on their own experiences. This chapter will discuss how to find and approach potential mentors, as well as how to make the most of the mentorship relationship. Having a mentor can help you navigate your career path more effectively and provide a sounding board for your ideas and challenges.

Networking etiquette and best practices will be covered in this chapter. It's essential to approach networking with a genuine and respectful attitude. Focus on building mutually beneficial relationships rather than simply seeking opportunities for yourself. This chapter will provide tips for professional communication, showing appreciation, and maintaining a positive reputation within your network. By practicing good networking etiquette, you'll build strong and lasting connections.

Chapter 8: Crafting a Winning Resume

Creating an effective resume that stands out is crucial in a competitive job market. Your resume is often the first impression you make on potential employers, so it's essential to make it count. This chapter will provide tips for crafting a compelling resume that highlights your achievements, skills, and experience. Focus on showcasing your unique value proposition and tailoring your resume to each job application.

Highlighting achievements and relevant experience is a key aspect of a winning resume. Use quantifiable metrics and specific examples to demonstrate your accomplishments. This chapter will guide you on how to effectively showcase your professional achievements and relate them to the job you're applying for. Highlighting your successes will make a strong case for why you're the best candidate for the position.

The role of cover letters and personal statements is often overlooked, but they can be powerful tools for making a lasting impression. A well-crafted cover letter can provide context for your resume and explain why you're passionate about the role and the company. This chapter will offer tips for writing compelling cover letters and personal statements that complement your resume and enhance your job application.

Tailoring applications for different job opportunities is essential for standing out in a competitive job market. Generic resumes and cover letters are less likely to catch the attention of hiring managers. This chapter will provide strategies for customizing your application materials for each job you apply to. By aligning your resume and cover letter with the specific requirements and culture of the company, you'll increase your chances of landing an interview.

Leveraging technology and professional resume services can give your job application an edge. Resume-building tools and templates can help you create a polished and professional-looking resume. Additionally, professional resume services can provide expert feedback and guidance to improve your application materials. This chapter will explore various resources and services available to help you craft a winning resume and stand out in the job market.

10

Chapter 9: Mastering the Job Search

Effective job search strategies and resources are essential for finding new opportunities. Start by identifying your career goals and creating a job search plan. Utilize job boards, company websites, and recruitment agencies to find job openings. Networking and attending industry events can also help you discover hidden opportunities. This chapter will provide a comprehensive guide to navigating the job market and finding the right opportunities for you.

Making the most of job boards, recruitment agencies, and networking events requires a proactive approach. Regularly update your online profiles and set up job alerts to stay informed about new openings. Attend career fairs and industry conferences to meet potential employers and learn about job opportunities. This chapter will offer tips for maximizing your job search efforts and increasing your chances of finding the right position.

Preparing for interviews is a crucial aspect of the job search process. Research the company, practice common interview questions, and prepare thoughtful questions to ask the interviewer. This chapter will provide strategies for acing interviews, including tips for building rapport, showcasing your skills, and demonstrating your enthusiasm for the role. Effective interview preparation can make a significant difference in your job search success.

Developing a personal brand and elevator pitch can help you stand out in a competitive job market. Your personal brand is a reflection of your skills, experience, and values, while your elevator pitch is a brief summary of who you are and what you bring to the table. This chapter will guide you through the process of crafting a compelling personal brand and elevator pitch that will make a strong impression on potential employers.

Staying motivated and organized during the job search process can be challenging, but it's essential for success. Set daily and weekly goals, track your applications, and follow up with employers. This chapter will offer tips for maintaining motivation, managing stress, and staying focused on your job search goals. With perseverance and a positive attitude, you can navigate the job search process and find the right opportunity for you.

11

Chapter 10: Thriving in the New Workplace

Adapting to a new work environment and culture is crucial for thriving in your new role. Take the time to learn about the company's values, expectations, and workplace dynamics. Building positive relationships with your new colleagues is essential for creating a supportive and collaborative work environment. This chapter will provide tips for successfully integrating into your new workplace and making a positive impact.

Building positive relationships with new colleagues involves effective communication, active listening, and mutual respect. Take the initiative to introduce yourself, participate in team activities, and offer your assistance when needed. This chapter will offer strategies for building strong professional relationships and creating a positive impression in your new workplace. Positive relationships can enhance your job satisfaction and career growth.

Balancing assertiveness and humility in a new role is important for gaining respect and building credibility. While it's essential to assert your ideas and contributions, it's also important to be open to feedback and willing to learn from others. This chapter will explore strategies for finding the right balance and navigating workplace dynamics with confidence and grace.

Setting boundaries and maintaining work-life balance is crucial for long-term success and well-being. Establishing clear boundaries between work and personal life can help prevent burnout and ensure you have time for relaxation and self-care. This chapter will provide tips for managing your workload, setting realistic expectations, and prioritizing your well-being. A healthy work-life balance is essential for sustained career success.

Continuous learning and growth in the new position are key to staying competitive and advancing your career. Seek opportunities for professional development, such as training programs, workshops, and mentorship. This chapter will emphasize the importance of ongoing learning and staying adaptable in a rapidly changing job market. By continuously improving your skills and knowledge, you can thrive in your new role and achieve long-term career success.

12

Chapter 11: Financial Planning After Dismissal

Managing finances during the transition period is essential for maintaining financial stability. Create a budget to track your expenses and prioritize essential needs. Look for ways to reduce costs and save money while you search for new employment. This chapter will provide practical tips for managing your finances during this challenging time, helping you navigate the transition with confidence.

Budgeting and saving strategies can help you make the most of your resources. Identify areas where you can cut back on non-essential expenses and focus on building an emergency fund. This chapter will offer strategies for creating a budget, managing debt, and finding ways to save money. Effective financial planning can provide peace of mind and ensure you have a safety net during the transition period.

Exploring alternative income sources and side hustles can provide additional financial support while you search for a new job. Consider freelance work, part-time jobs, or gig opportunities to supplement your income. This chapter will explore various options for earning extra money and provide tips for balancing multiple income streams. Diversifying your income sources can help you stay financially stable and reduce stress.

Planning for long-term financial goals is essential for ensuring future security and stability. Set realistic financial goals and create a plan to achieve them. This chapter will guide you through the process of setting short-term and long-term financial goals, such as saving for retirement, investing, and building wealth. By planning for the future, you can create a solid financial foundation and achieve your financial aspirations.

Seeking professional financial advice can provide valuable insights and guidance. Financial advisors can help you create a comprehensive financial plan, manage investments, and navigate complex financial decisions. This chapter will discuss the benefits of seeking professional advice and provide tips for finding a reputable financial advisor. With expert guidance, you can make informed financial decisions and achieve long-term success.

13

Chapter 12: Embracing the Journey

Reflecting on the personal and professional growth achieved during this journey is an important step in moving forward. Take the time to acknowledge the challenges you've overcome and the progress you've made. This chapter will encourage you to celebrate your achievements and recognize the resilience and strength you've developed. Reflecting on your growth can provide a sense of accomplishment and motivate you to continue striving for success.

Embracing the new chapter with confidence and optimism is essential for a successful transition. View this experience as an opportunity for growth and new beginnings. This chapter will emphasize the importance of maintaining a positive attitude and focusing on the possibilities that lie ahead. By embracing change with an open mind and a hopeful outlook, you can create a brighter future for yourself.

Maintaining a positive attitude and resilient mindset is crucial for overcoming challenges and achieving your goals. Practice gratitude, stay connected with your support network, and engage in activities that bring you joy and fulfillment. This chapter will provide tips for cultivating a positive mindset and building resilience in the face of adversity. A positive attitude can enhance your well-being and drive you toward success.

Sharing the journey and experiences with others can provide valuable support and inspiration. By opening up about your challenges and successes, you can create meaningful connections and support others who may be going through similar experiences. This chapter will discuss the benefits of sharing your journey and offer tips for connecting with others. Sharing your story can provide a sense of purpose and contribute to a supportive community.

Looking forward to future opportunities and successes is an essential part of embracing the journey. Stay focused on your goals, continue to seek new opportunities, and remain open to change. This chapter will encourage you to keep moving forward with confidence and optimism. By staying proactive and adaptable, you can create a successful and fulfilling future.

Next Chapter: Getting Better After Dismissal is a comprehensive guide designed to help individuals navigate the challenging journey of recovering from job dismissal. This book offers practical advice, emotional support, and inspiration to turn this life-altering event into a transformative experience.

Starting with the initial shock and emotional turmoil that often accompanies dismissal, the book addresses the complex range of emotions one might feel. It encourages readers to acknowledge their feelings and provides strategies for coping with stress and building emotional resilience. By embracing vulnerability and seeking support from loved ones, readers will find the strength to move forward.

Self-reflection and learning from past experiences are key themes in this book. Through honest self-assessment and constructive feedback, readers can identify areas for improvement and turn mistakes into valuable learning opportunities. The book emphasizes the importance of a growth mindset and provides a roadmap for personal and professional development.

Rebuilding confidence and redefining success are crucial steps in the recovery process. The book offers practical tips for setting achievable goals, celebrating small victories, and maintaining a positive attitude. It encourages readers to explore new career paths and align their professional aspirations with their personal values. By adopting a growth mindset, readers can embrace change and find fulfillment in new ventures.

Networking and building a strong support system are also highlighted in the book. Readers will learn strategies for expanding their professional network, leveraging social media, and finding mentorship. The book underscores the importance of meaningful connections and provides tips for maintaining positive relationships in the workplace.

Financial planning during the transition period is another essential topic covered in this book. Readers will find practical advice on budgeting, saving, exploring alternative income sources, and seeking professional financial guidance. By managing their finances effectively, readers can ensure financial stability and plan for future success.

Finally, **Next Chapter: Getting Better After Dismissal** encourages readers to embrace the journey with confidence and optimism. It emphasizes the importance of continuous learning, maintaining a positive attitude, and sharing experiences with others. By focusing on personal growth and staying proactive, readers can turn their dismissal into an opportunity for growth and success.

This book is a supportive companion for anyone facing the challenges of job dismissal. It offers a blend of practical advice, emotional support, and inspiration to help readers navigate this difficult period and emerge stronger and more determined.

www.ingramcontent.com/pod-product-compliance
Lightning Source LLC
LaVergne TN
LVHW020742090526
838202LV00057BA/6182